Autumn and Winter Activities Come Rain or Shine

Seasonal Crafts and Games for Children

Edited by Stefanie Pfister

Floris
Books

Contents

Winter

Foreword

Children love to play inside and outside, and with nature, whatever the weather – come rain or shine. They want to help garden birds in winter by building feeders and nesting boxes. They enjoy making beautiful decorations from natural objects like sticks, pine cones, feathers, seeds and leaves. They love playing outdoors in the snow and building bonfires in the woods. They are inquisitive, inventive and daring.

This collection of indoor and outdoor nature activities has been compiled out of ideas and questions from curious children, with the aim of offering practical ways to learn about and create with nature.

Each activity includes detailed instructions for you to follow, as well as natural science sections explaining the phenomena that children often ask about: who has been nibbling pine cones in the forest? Which tracks in the snow belong to which animal? How can we navigate using the night sky in wintertime?

This book includes a range of activities for all the family to enjoy: some suitable for children as young as four, others more suited to older children. Parents, grandparents and teachers can also join in the fun while experiencing the wonders of the natural world.

Autumn

Playing with Leaves

Have fun in the brightly coloured forest

Many leaves turn yellow, orange, red and brown in autumn, while some fall to the ground when they're still green. The mixture of colours makes our woods and forests look so pretty!

When the ground is covered with leaves it's fun to run and jump through them and listen to them rustle. You could gather a big pile of leaves for hedgehogs to hibernate in over winter. Try sliding down a leaf-covered bank, but watch out for sticks and stones hiding under the soft leaves!

Tie colourful leaves to a jam jar with a ribbon to make an attractive autumn lantern

Why do leaves change colour?

The leaves on trees change colour depending on their location in the world, the time of year, the weather and their genetic properties. A chemical called chlorophyll absorbs energy from sunlight in spring and summer and gives leaves their green colour. But in autumn, it breaks down and the leaves turn yellow, orange and red colours.

The leaves of different trees become different colours, for example: hornbeam, lime (linden) and birch leaves all turn yellow; oak leaves turn brown; and maple, rose and dogwood leaves turn a mixture of colours.

The breakdown of colour ends when the leaves turn brown. Before leaves fall off a tree, a protective seal is produced between the leaf stem and the tree, which prevents fungi and pests from entering.

13

Clay Village

Build houses out of soft, smooth clay

You can use either natural clay or modelling clay to build your village. Modelling clay is sold in most craft shops. Natural clay can be found by the banks of streams, and is made up of clay, silt and sand. The more clay in the mixture, the easier it will be to mould and the better it will harden.

First of all, find a weatherproof place to build your village; it will collapse if it gets wet.

If you're using natural clay, mould it into a square or rectangular block. Modelling clay usually comes in this shape, but you may need to wet it slightly to make it more flexible.

Tie a length of thin string between two small sticks to make a clay cutter. If you wrap the string around the block, cross the sticks over and pull, the thread will slice through the clay.

Use your cutter to slice four walls and two roof slabs for each house. Stand the walls up and press the edges together firmly, then smooth the joins using a sculpting tool or your fingers.

When all four walls are standing securely, add the roof slabs, pressing all the joins together securely and smoothing the edges well.

Cut windows and doors out using a blunt knife or the pointed end of the sculpting tool.

15

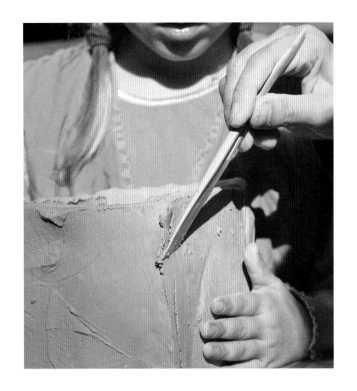

Using the broken tiles, bark branches and any other decorations you have found, tile the roof and decorate the windows. It is better to use only one material to tile the roof, so it looks like a proper house, for example only rosehips or only spruce branches. Carefully press each piece into the roof clay.

Make a ridge for the roof from a different material, such as stones on a moss roof or a twig on a tiled roof.

Arrange the clay houses on a bed of moss or leaves, and make roads and paths between the houses from gravel, sticks or bark.

If you make 24 houses you can use your clay village as an Advent calendar. You can even build a church for Christmas Eve and place a tealight inside.

Acorn Chain

Make a hanging decoration from felt acorns

You will need

To make two large leaves, two small leaves and five acorns:

- felting-wool batting: approximately 15–20 g (½ oz) olive green, 2 g (a pinch) dark green, 10 g (¼ oz) light brown, 5 g (a pinch) chestnut
- real acorn cups
- small twigs, including 1 long thin twig, such as elder
- gold or beige embroidery thread
- embroidery needle
- bowl of warm soapy water
- bubble wrap
- knitting needle
- glue

Felting the leaves

To make the leaves, wet felt a piece of flat felt using olive-coloured wool. Start by pulling palm-sized pieces of olive-green wool out of the batting. Place these pieces on the bubble wrap, like overlapping tiles, to make a square of approximately 20 x 20 cm (8 x 8 in). Add a second layer, positioned at a right angle to the one just laid. Add darker green fibres to the third and final olive-green layer. Wet it all with warm soapy water.

With wet hands, rub the wool in gentle circular movements from the outside of the square towards the centre. Be careful not to pull the layers apart while felting. Work with increasing pressure until the layers are combined and keep adding water as you go. Turn the piece of felt over, wet the other side and repeat the process.

To 'full' the felt, wet it again with soapy water and knead it like dough. Roll it up several times with increasing pressure. Once the felt sheet feels completely combined, stroke it smooth with your hand. Rinse it well with clean water and leave it to dry.

When the felt sheet is dry, cut out leaves using the templates to help you.

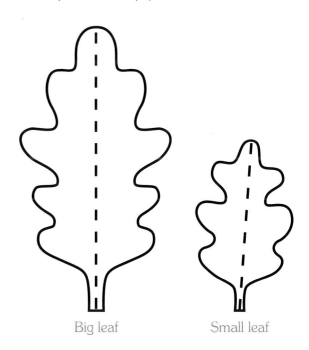

Big leaf   Small leaf

Using soapy water, felt the cut edge of the leaves into shape. Rinse them with clean water and let them dry. Use embroidery thread to sew on veins.

Felting the acorns

To make the acorns, tease some chestnut and light-brown wool together.

Pull two thin strands from the mixed wool – not too long or your acorn will be too big. Tie a knot in the centre of one strip. Wind the overhanging ends around the knot to form the acorn shape. Place the second strand crosswise over it and wind the ends around to build your acorn. It should be about one third larger then the real acorn cup you will attach to the top.

Immerse the woollen acorn in warm soapy water until it's saturated. Carefully squeeze out any excess water and start felting gently. Roll the acorn in circular movements from all sides using your hands until it is oval in shape.

Once the acorn feels firm enough, roll it on all sides on the bubble wrap, using increasing pressure and plenty of soapy water.

To finish, rinse with clean water and leave to dry.

Glue the acorn cup in place at the top of your felt acorn.

Making the chain

Push out the marrow of the elder stick using a knitting needle and cut it into small tubular 'beads'.

Use embroidery thread to join all the elements together, sewing through the felt pieces and elder beads, wrapping thread around twig bundles, and carefully pushing through the acorn and its cup with a sharp pointed needle.

Make a loop at the top to hang up your decoration.

Tip: Make extra leaves and use them as gift or bag tags.

Place felt acorns in real acorn cups

Nutty Crafts

Use wild nuts to create and decorate

When the sun shines through the golden leaves of a majestic chestnut tree, search the base of its trunk for prickly seed husks. What's inside? A shiny brown conker of course! Take a bag and collect as many as you can. Look out for acorns too. You can use these to make small animals and figures, or to decorate picture frames.

Tip: Ask an adult to help if you're using a glue gun or hand drill.

Make conker caterpillars, table decorations and leaf plates for a pretend autumn picnic

Making pressed-leaf pictures

You will need

- pretty autumn leaves
- heavy books
- plain paper
- greaseproof paper
- coloured cardboard
- glue
- picture frame

Find a heavy book and open it near the middle. Line one page with greaseproof paper then plain paper, and place some pretty leaves on top. Add another sheet of plain paper followed by greaseproof, then close the book to squash the leaves between the pages. The greaseproof paper will protect the book from any liquid that comes out of the leaves.

Place the book under a few other heavy books and leave them for up to four weeks. Smaller leaves may take less time to dry than larger ones. You can check by gently peeling away the edge of the papers to see if the leaves are dry. Once you're sure the leaves are ready, gently peel away the rest of the paper.

Glue your leaves onto a cardboard background to make a pretty picture. Cut the card to fit a ready-made frame, or make your own!

Making and decorating frames

You will need

- 🌸 acorns and conkers
- 🌸 string or ribbon
- 🌸 a glue gun
- 🌸 twigs or long sections of bark

Acorns and conkers make good decorations for wooden picture frames.

To make your own frame, lay sticks or bark together in a square or rectangle (or any shape you like) to form the frame, then glue them together.

Next add decorations, such as acorns or conkers. Acorns fall out of their cups when they dry, so glue them together before you use them. Conkers get lighter and are easier to attach when they dry out, so wait a couple of days before you glue them on.

Leave your frame to dry, then glue it on top of your chosen picture and leave it to dry once more.

Tie on a piece of string or ribbon to hang up your frame.

Creating conker creatures

You will need

- shells and acorn cups
- matches or toothpicks
- pen

To make a *caterpillar*, choose four or five conkers for the body and one for the head.

Use a hand drill to bore small holes in the conkers, deep enough to keep a matchstick secure. Link the conkers together using matchsticks or toothpicks.

Drill a second hole on the top of the end body conker, and attach the head.

Draw on eyes, nose and a smile, and glue on an acorn cup for a hat.

To make a *hedgehog*, use one large conker for the body and drill a hole in one side. For the head, drill another hole in a slightly smaller conker and attach it to the large one.

Glue a dried conker shell onto the body for spikes and draw on eyes. Glue on an acorn cup to make a snout.

Use dried conker shells to add prickles to hedgehogs and caterpillars

Hedgehog meets beetle – make a nature park on your windowsill

What's the difference between sweet chestnuts and horse chestnuts?

The sweet chestnut (*Castanea sativa*) and horse chestnut (*Aesculus hippocastanum*) trees have nothing in common apart from their name. The chestnuts we eat are the fruit of the sweet chestnut tree, but we can't eat the fruit of horse chestnut trees, which we know as conkers. In the past, horses were given horse chestnuts to ease a cough, which is how they got their name.

Horse chestnut trees have large hand-shaped leaves and white candle-like flowers. These beautiful trees are often planted in avenues. After the blossoms have wilted the fruit grows inside its prickly husk, splitting open in autumn to reveal the treasure within. Conkers left lying on the ground make nutritious food for wild animals in winter, so don't collect them all!

Feather Crafts

Gather beautiful feathers to make Native American style accessories

Large or small, fluffy or sleek, colourful or plain, feathers vary for different types of bird. Some have distinctive markings, like peacock feathers. Some are more generic, such as seagulls or pigeons. A male mallard duck – the drake – has glossy blue and green feathers in contrast to the brown female. Within each species, every bird has different markings.

Feathers can be used for many things. In the past, Native American used colourful feathers to decorate their headwear and clothing and to stabilise their arrows. Before fountain pens were invented, people used feathers as quills, dipping them in ink to write. Today, feathers are still used to decorate festive hats, stuff pillows and duvets, and to decorate clothes.

Birds lose more feathers when they moult in summer and autumn, so that's the best time to look for them. But you can also find them in winter and spring when the fields and forests are bare, revealing feathers that might have been hidden under summer leaves. Moulting happens to replace old feathers: new ones grow that push the old ones out. Moulting takes a lot of energy, so birds wait for summer or autumn when plenty of food is available.

Birds have different types of feathers: wing feathers are specially constructed for flying, tail feathers help with steering and braking, and some are waterproof. Contour feathers can be seen from the outside and give birds their typical shape; they also keep birds warm by trapping air between two layers; and they can be ruffled

A pheasant's breast feathers

A pheasant's tail feathers

25

to stop heat building up, keeping birds cool. By looking at the shape of a contour feather, we can find out where on the bird it's from: tail feathers are usually symmetrical with the rigid shaft running down the centre, but wing feathers are often asymmetrical.

We're most likely to find contour feathers as they are robust and can withstand damp and dirt. Their fine structure can be seen with the naked eye, but try looking closer with a magnifying glass. On both sides of the hard shaft there are barbs made out of tiny, branched feathers, which hold together thanks to little hooks that attach like Velcro. If the branched feathers rip apart, they can easily be repaired when the bird smoothes its plumage with its beak. Try it yourself by smoothing a dishevelled feather with your fingers.

Pigeon feather

A buzzard's wing feather

26

Making a feather pendant

You will need

- small feather
- thin craft wire, leather thong or string
- wooden beads

Find a small feather that will make a pretty pendant. Secure the shaft of the feather to the end of a piece of wire, leather thong or string.

Thread wooden beads onto the wire or string and then onto the shaft of the feather. Secure the end to stop the beads falling off, but leave a small section free so that you can tie it to a key, bag or necklace.

To make a necklace, take a longer piece of wire, leather thong or string, and thread on beads in your preferred pattern. After threading your last beads, tie the ends together. Tie or twist your feather pendant onto your necklace.

Making a feather propeller

You will need

- 2 feathers, roughly the same size
- cork ball
- long wooden stick

Find two feathers that are roughly the same size, push them into either side of a cork ball and insert a long stick into the bottom of the ball. Lift the stick, with the feather propeller at the top, as high as you can and twist it quickly between your palms. Will it fly?

Drawing portraits

You will need

- feathers
- paper
- oil pastels
- masking tape

Using paper and oil pastels draw the head and shoulders of a person. Stick feathers onto the headdress with masking tape. You could even glue on single feathers for earrings. Use long pheasant feathers or more unusual feathers for the Chief to show how important he is.

Tying braids

You will need

- small fluffy feathers
- craft wire or coloured yarn

Small fluffy feathers make attractive hair accessories. Thread feathers onto thin craft wire or tie them onto coloured yarn, then plait your feathery adornment into your hair.

Making a Chief's staff

You will need

- feathers
- a big stick, preferably with wormholes
- a hand drill

Find a big stick, preferably one with lots of useful wormholes. Alternatively, you can use a hand drill to make your own holes. Push feathers into the holes to decorate your staff. Now you are Chief!

Writing with feathers

You will need

- feathers
- craft knife
- small pot of paint
- paper

To make a quill, carefully cut the end of a feather with a craft knife to make a point. Ask an adult if you need help with this!

Dip the pointed end into a small pot of paint and try writing on a piece of paper. Keep dipping your quill to top up the paint.

Leave your letters and pictures to dry.

Playing Native American tribes

Once you have used all your feathers to make accessories and props, you can gather your friends and start a tribe!

Start by choosing a name for your tribe, such as 'People of the Wind' or 'Big Hare People'. Try taking inspiration from the natural world around you. Each member of the tribe can then choose their own name, such as 'Little Green Leaf' or 'Water Child'.

You could write each other secret messages using your feather quills, or sneak through the forest in search of another tribe. Once you have spotted them, greet them with loud whoops and cheers!

How many feathers do birds have?

From left to right: a pheasant tail feather, a wild goose wing feather, a buzzard wing feather, a pigeon feather, a small pheasant feather, a duck feather, and a small buzzard feather

Different birds need different amounts of feathers. A little house sparrow has about 1,400, a small duck has about 11,000 and a big swan has about 25,000 feathers. No two feathers are the same – but when arranged together, they give each bird its typical appearance. A single feather is just one piece in the bigger plumage puzzle.

Making Natural Jewellery

Create bracelets and necklaces from dried seeds and nuts

You will need

- seeds and nuts, such as apple, pear and melon pips, acorns, beechnuts
- section of thin hollow twig
- small pieces of straw
- embroidery thread or thin craft wire
- twine
- embroidery needle
- food colouring
- small bowls and boxes
- scissors
- thimble
- metal jewellery fasteners

It will take several weeks to collect enough nut and seed beads. Keep each type of bead in a small box and once you have gathered enough you can begin.

Thread your needle with thin wire or embroidery thread. To make a necklace you will need a long section, but a bracelet can be shorter.

Some seeds, such as apple, pear and melon pips, are easier to sew through when they're fresh and soft. Acorns and acorn cups are more difficult to pierce, so use a thimble or ask an adult to help you.

1, 2, 3, 4... How many apple pips can you collect?

String acorn cups up carefully as they can easily break

Beechnut shells make pretty pendants if knotted on tightly

This time there are 5 pips in the apple and 6 in the pear

34

Thread on short lengths of hollow twig or straw to make different patterns. You can also tie beechnuts or carefully push the needle through the stalk.

When you've finished, tie a metal fastener to each end and you're done!

Why not try dyeing lighter coloured seeds before threading to make more colourful jewellery? Leave the seeds in small bowls filled with food colouring for a week, drain them and then leave them to dry out.

Use a thimble for tricky threading – acorns are the most difficult to sew through

You can use an old cheese box to store your jewellery!

A pear-seed and beechnut bracelet

Stick Crafts

Create artwork, decorations and a catapult from sticks

Making a stick picture

You will need

- sticks of varying sizes
- coloured yarn or string
- feathers and berries
- strong glue

Lay four sticks out in a square or rectangle shape to make the frame and tie them together at the corners with yarn or string.

Glue or tie small sticks together to make a picture to go inside the frame. You could make a house or ladder, as shown here, or maybe a kite or star? You could add your favourite forest finds as well – beautiful feathers or berries. Then tie all your picture elements to the frame.

Making a stick star

You will need

- 6 sticks the same size
- coloured yarn or string
- strong glue

Make a triangle using three sticks of the same length and tie the ends together with coloured yarn.

Repeat this step, then place the two triangles over each other to make a six-pointed star. Tie or glue the two stars together.

Attach a loop of yarn or string to the top and hang the star decoration from your window or Christmas tree.

Making a catapult

You will need

- sturdy v-shaped stick
- strong elastic band
- small piece of leather or strong fabric
- fabric scissors or craft knife
- pieces of paper, peas or conkers

Find a sturdy stick with a 'V' shape at the top – the perfect stick for a catapult!

Carefully cut a strong elastic band to make a long strip of elastic. If there is a flap on it, position that at the centre to hold your ammunition. Alternatively, carefully cut two parallel slits in a piece of leather or strong fabric – ask an adult to help! Thread the elastic through the slits, then tie each end of the elastic to a prong of the stick.

Now you can practise firing your catapult, but always do so away from breakable objects, windows, animals and other people! Start with scrunched-up pieces of paper, then as your aim gets better you can try shooting with harder items such as peas or conkers.

Making stick torches and candle holders

You will need

- sticks of varying sizes
- clay pot with a hole in the bottom
- candles
- floral foam (Oasis)
- string

Make stick torches and table decorations for an autumn party

Tip: Always ask an adult to help light candles, and be extremely careful when the candles are alight.

To make a *stick torch*, fill a clay pot with floral foam and push a thick candle securely into the centre.

Push a long sturdy stick through the hole in the bottom of the clay pot into the floral foam. This will be your torch handle.

Arrange a variety of twigs and sticks around the outside of the pot, not too close to the candle.

Secure them tightly in place with a length of string, winding it round several times.

Find a sheltered place, away from the wind, and push your torch into the ground. When it gets dark, light the candle.

To make a *candle holder*, fill a clay pot with floral foam and push long candles into the centre.

Break sticks into different lengths – shorter than the candles so they don't catch light when the candles are lit. Push the sticks into the foam around the candles.

Leafy Tablecloth

Make an unusual tablecloth for autumn picnics

You will need

- dried autumn leaves
- hessian fabric, an old tablecloth, or other thick fabric
- glue gun

Oak leaves make a glowing bronze tablecloth

Spread the fabric out on a heatproof surface. It needs to be thick so that the glue doesn't soak through and stick to the work surface.

Using a glue gun, stick the dried leaves in place. Layer them like fish scales to avoid gaps.

Leave your creation to dry, then spread it over an outdoor table. Your leaf tablecloth will stay pretty throughout the winter.

Forest Cone Creatures

Make animals and gnomes from pine, fir and spruce cones

You will need

- conifer cones (pine, spruce, fir) of varying sizes
- small twigs and sticks
- acorn cups
- small pieces of cone or bark
- sheep's wool, natural bast fibre or knitting yarn
- strong glue, ideally a glue gun
- red, white and black waterproof pens
- dried berries
- unshelled nuts, such as hazelnuts

Making fir or spruce-cone sheep

Glue four small twigs to the underside of a long fir or spruce cone to make legs.

Wind the wool, bast fibre or knitting yarn generously around the cone, leaving the pointed end free for the head. This will be the woolly body.

Break off small pieces of cone or bark and glue them on as ears. Use acorn cups or berries for a nose, and draw on eyes with waterproof pens.

Make a stable from a wooden box lined with hay to keep your sheep warm in winter

Making pine-cone gnomes

Stand a cone on the wide end with the pointed end at the top. Glue small twig arms to the top of the cone and leave it to dry.

Glue on a nut for a head and draw on eyes, nose and a mouth using waterproof pens.

Use sheep's wool, berries, acorn cups and bark to decorate your gnome. You could give it a bark and berry hat, a woollen scarf or acorn-cup buttons.

Give your gnomes hats, scarves and buttons

42

Forest cone eaters

Many animals and birds eat the cones that grow on evergreen conifer trees, especially in winter. The hard cone scales are not nutritious, but the seeds inside contain valuable fat, starch and protein. It's difficult to get past the protective scales to reach the delicious seeds, so creatures need to either lift up or remove each one in their own special way.

Squirrels eat up high

Squirrels eat their cones high up in the trees so they can watch out for predators while they feed. They pull off the scales to reach the seeds inside, then they eat from the bottom up until all that's left is the frayed tip, which the squirrel holds while eating.

Mice hide away

Mice often hide when they're eating so nothing disturbs them, which makes it hard to find out where they've been. Mice bite cone scales off with their sharp teeth, leaving behind a smooth stalk.

Woodpeckers are clever

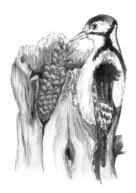

Woodpeckers wedge the tips of cones into crevices in trees to hold them in place while they eat. They peck hard to reach the seeds below the scales, and usually eat from the top down, leaving the leftover stalk looking quite dishevelled.

Who has picked the pine cone clean?

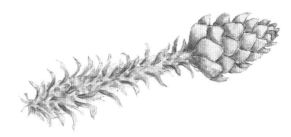

Squirrels leave the tip

Mice leave a smooth stalk

Woodpeckers leave the scales and peck down below to get the seeds

When you're on a woodland walk, look closely at the cones on the ground. You can tell which animals have been feeding there from the stalk and remaining scales.

Cone-producing conifers

Pine or larch, spruce or fir? You can identify each type of conifer tree by looking at its needles and cones.

Spruce tree

Spruce cones are long and hang down from branches. They only stand up when they are young, red and soft, but once mature, they droop downwards and eventually fall off the tree. Spruce needles feel prickly and are attached to twigs by small, stalk-like woody projections. If you remove the needles, the twigs feel rough.

Fir tree

Fir cones are long and stand upright on branches like candles. As they mature, the scales fall off the centre stalk of the cone down to the ground. Fir needles feel soft and are attached to the twig by a unique base, similar to a suction cup. If you remove the needles, the twigs feel smooth. If you are struggling to tell the difference between spruce and fir, remember that fir needles feel soft, while spruce needles feel prickly.

Pine tree

Pine cones are egg-shaped. They fall to the ground intact, rather than dropping individual seeds. Pine needles grow in pairs and are very long.

Larch tree

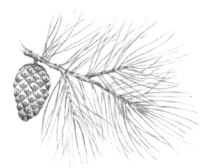

The larch is the only tree in the conifer family that loses its needles in winter, but the small, egg-shaped cones stay on the branches all season long. Larch needles grow in small bunches and turn golden yellow in autumn. They emit a mild citrus smell when rubbed. But beware! Larch needles are slightly poisonous, whereas fir, spruce and pine needles are not.

Potato Bonfire

Bake delicious potatoes on a bonfire made from old potato plants

Building a potato bonfire

You will need

* fallen branches and logs
* dried potato plants
* matches or a lighter
* newspaper to make a taper

Tip: Always ask an adult to help you when lighting and maintaining a bonfire.

Autumn is the perfect season to gather potatoes and bake them in a crackling bonfire. How delicious they will taste fresh out of the embers!

First, you'll need to search the forest for fallen wood to build your fire, and logs for people to sit on around the bonfire.

Next, light some of the dried potato plants and push them into gaps in your firewood to set it alight. Alternatively, push the potato plants in first, then roll up a sheet of newspaper to make a taper and use it to light the potato plants. It may take a little while for the bonfire to get going, but once it does it will be smoky!

Potato holidays

In the past, children in rural communities in the UK, Germany and Scandinavia were given time off school for 'potato holidays' ('tattie holidays' in Scotland) during October, when they would harvest potatoes each day for a week. This was an arduous task and farmers were grateful for every helping hand. In Germany, after the work was done, the dry potato plants were raked together, thrown into several heaps and burned. This eliminated plant diseases such as blight, as the fire burned away any bacteria or viruses that might harm future crops.

The dry leaves make a lovely fire, and in clear weather during this October week you could see the flames shining over the fields and smell the bitter smoke plumes. The potato fire was the highlight of the holiday, when children would collect any leftover potatoes from the fields and throw them in the flames to cook. Delicious!

Baking potatoes in a bonfire

You will need

- baking potatoes
- clay
- garden fork
- long stick
- pointed stick or wooden skewer
- spoon or fork to eat with
- pocket knife
- paper plates and napkins
- heatproof gloves

Once the fire has died down and the flames have gone, you can bake potatoes in the embers. If you cook them in the flames they will burn on the outside but still be hard inside.

Using heatproof gloves, carefully drop the potatoes into the embers and leave them until the skin is burned. Alternatively, you could skewer a potato on a pointed stick and hold it in the embers to cook. Use a long stick or garden fork to turn them every so often to make sure they are baked all the way through.

Once they are done, carefully remove the potatoes from the fire using a garden fork or long stick and let them cool a little. Peel off the burned crusts, halve the potatoes with a pocket knife and let the insides cool a little more before you eat them.

You can grow your own potatoes by planting a 'seed' potato in the ground then, when a new plant has grown, dig up the new potatoes

Clay-baked potatoes

If you don't want the potato skins to burn, you can cover them in clay before placing them in the embers. Turn them every so often to make sure they are baked all the way through.

When the clay coverings have hardened, lift the potatoes out of the fire with a garden fork or a pointed stick. Let them cool a little before you break open the clay.

Cut the potatoes in half with a pocket knife and enjoy them, skin and all.

You could carve your own wooden spoon using a pocket knife and use it to eat your potato

The history of the potato

Potatoes originate from the Andes mountain range in South America. Sailors first brought them to Europe in the sixteenth century, and Sir Francis Drake is commonly credited for introducing the potato to England. At first the aristocracy admired these exotic plants for their beautiful flowers, so the plant was grown in botanic gardens. Gradually the use of potato plants evolved from being ornamental to being one of the most important foods in the western world.

In eighteenth century Prussia (now part of Germany), Frederick the Great started growing potatoes on a large scale after war and famine left his people starving. Until that point, farmers in northern Europe had only grown grain as a staple food. The potato began to grow in popularity due to its ease of growth, cost-effectiveness and its ability to satisfy hunger.

In Ireland, the potato provided a perfect crop for the poor to grow on small plots: an acre of potatoes and the milk from one cow was enough to feed a whole Irish family. By the mid-nineteenth century, the potato made up approximately one third of all crops grown in Ireland. But disaster struck between 1845–49 when blight attacked the Irish potato harvest, leading to terrible famine and approximately one million deaths. In the following years, around another million Irish citizens emigrated to Britain, the USA and Canada, among other places.

Forest Musical Instruments

Play beautiful music using nuts and sticks

Make your own musical instruments and gather your friends for a concert. Use a long stick to play wood chimes, or make higher notes on a willow flute. Knocking, rattling, whistling and dinging: gentle sounds will soon ring alongside the natural noises of the forest.

Tip: These activities involve sawing, drilling and whittling so ask an adult to help you.

Making nut rattles

You will need

- nutshells (walnut) and conkers
- sticks
- wire
- small drill

Walnut rattle

Open some walnuts very carefully so the shell halves remain intact. Remove the nuts and drill a small hole through the centre of each shell half. Ask an adult to help you use the drill.

Thread the shells onto a length of wire as if you were making a necklace. For the best sound, place two halves of the same shell facing each other.

Nutshell and conker rattle

Find a straight stick to make the handle of your rattle.

Drill holes through the conkers and nutshells and thread each one onto its own length of wire, fixing them at one end.

Fasten the other end of each wire to one end of a straight stick. They will hold better if you make small notches in the stick or drill a small hole to thread the wires through.

Twist or swirl the stick so the shells and conkers bang together.

Making wood chimes

You will need

- 2 sturdy tree trunks growing close together
- 1 long branch to tie between the tree trunks
- 5 different size branches (in thickness and length) for the chimes
- 1 branch for a drumstick
- strong wire
- wire-cutters
- rope or coconut string
- strong hooks, bent nails or staples (to hold wood)
- hammer
- small drill
- saw

Wrap strong wire around the ends of the long branch and position it horizontally between the two tree trunks. If you want to protect the trees from damage, wrap coconut string around the wire before fixing the branch in place.

Saw the chime branches into different lengths and widths so they make a range of different notes. The thicker the branch, the lower the sound; the thinner the branch, the higher the sound. You could saw the branches vertically – very carefully – if you want to make them thinner.

To hang your chimes, attach hooks or staples to one end. Sort them by length – shortest to longest – then use the wire to hang them from the long branch between the tree trunks. Wind coconut string around the wire.

Find another branch to use as drumstick to sound the chimes.

Whittling a flute

You will need

- freshly cut (pussy) willow or rowan-tree twig about 8–10 cm (3–4 in) long and roughly 1–2 cm (¾ in) in diameter
- sharp pocket knife

You will need to take a few factors into account when choosing a twig. Firstly, the thicker the twig, the lower the sound your flute will make; the thinner the flute, the higher the sound. Secondly, you will need a long stretch of smooth twig to make the flute, so make sure any buds or knots are spaced far apart.

Start by cutting the twig off cleanly, approximately three-finger spaces above a knot at the thicker end of the stick.

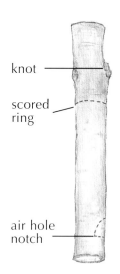

knot

scored ring

air hole notch

1. Score a ring around the bark below the knot, but don't cut the twig itself. Cut a notch for the air hole in the bark at the lower end of the twig.

air hole

2. Tap above the air-hole notch using the handle of the pocket knife to soften it, rotating as you tap. Remove the bark by holding tight at the top end and twisting back and forth until it loosens. Then carefully slip the bark with the air hole off the twig. This is not easy!

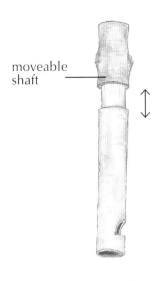

moveable shaft

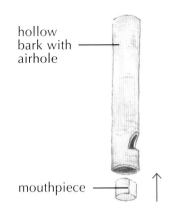

hollow bark with airhole

mouthpiece

3. Push the bark back onto the twig.

5. Push the mouthpiece back into the hollow bark.

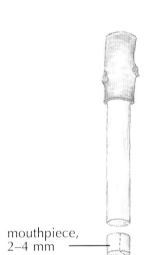

mouthpiece, 2–4 mm

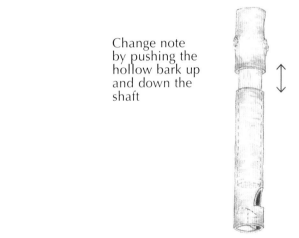

Change note by pushing the hollow bark up and down the shaft

4. Mark a point for cutting the mouthpiece with the knife. Pull off the bark with the air hole and cut the twig at the marked place to make your mouthpiece. Cut an approximately 2–4 mm ($^2/_{16}$–$^3/_{16}$ in) thin strip lengthways off the mouthpiece.

6. Push the bark back onto the flute. Now you can blow through it!

Unfortunately, after a few hours the bark will dry out so the flute will not keep forever. If you place the twig in water it will last a little longer.

Making a corn-cob guiro

You will need

- ⚘ ripe cob of corn
- ⚘ a small stick

Buy a ripe cob of corn from a shop, or if you grow your own or know a corn farmer, ask if you can pick one. Remove the leaves and leave it to dry indoors for a few days.

When the corn is hard, use the stick to rub up and down on the cob. The harder the corn, the louder your guiro will be.

Autumn Lanterns

Make glowing lanterns from turnips and leaves

Add a bright glow to dark autumn evenings with homemade lanterns. Make sure you dress warmly if you're going outside in the chilly autumn weather, and keep lanterns out of the wind so they don't blow out.

St Martin's Day

In many European countries people celebrate St Martin's Day (or Martinmas) on November 11 to honour St Martin of Tours, who was born in the fourth century AD in what is now Hungary. According to legend, as a soldier he gave his cloak to a poor man to save him from freezing. Later he became Bishop of Tours, in France, and after his death he was made a saint. The tradition of processing with lanterns on an evening walk was started in the 19th century. Each tiny fragile light, working together to brighten the darkness, symbolises the importance of small acts of kindness in our world, as displayed by St Martin. Schools and nurseries often start making lanterns in early November.

Making a pumpkin lantern

You will need

- round, even pumpkin or turnip
- sharp knife
- spoon
- straight stick

Tip: Ask an adult to help you use the sharp knife.

Even when a pumpkin or turnip is hollowed out it is very heavy, so this project may be more suitable for older children. Or young children can ask someone to carry the lantern for them.

Slice off the top of the pumpkin then carve it out using a knife and spoon. When it's hollow, carve eyes, a nose and a mouth.

Sharpen one end of the straight stick and carefully push it into the bottom of the pumpkin as a handle.

Place a tealight into the hollow pumpkin head to light it up.

Making a leaf lantern

You will need

- balloon
- colourful leaves (thicker leaves work well)
- wallpaper paste or white craft glue
- paintbrush
- baking parchment or greaseproof paper
- wire
- thick needle
- stick for holding the lantern

Blow up a balloon and place it somewhere it won't roll around.

Rip the baking parchment into small pieces.

Cover the balloon with wallpaper paste or craft glue and stick a layer of torn paper onto it. Don't glue right up to the knot. Layer more glue onto the paper and stick a layer of leaves on top. Make sure the leaves don't overlap too much so the light can shine through.

Prop the balloon somewhere it won't roll to dry for a couple of days. Once dry, pop the balloon with a needle and pull the balloon pieces gently away.

Pierce two holes in the top of the lantern at opposite sides using the needle. Loop wire through these holes and fasten the wire to the stick.

Place a tealight in the lantern and watch it glow.

Lantern Song

I go with my little lantern,
my lantern goes with me.

In Heaven the stars are shining,
down here on Earth shine we.

Shine your light through the still dark night,
A-bim-a-la-bam-a-la-boom.

The lights grow dim, we must go in,
A-bim-a-la-bam-a-la-boom.

Winter

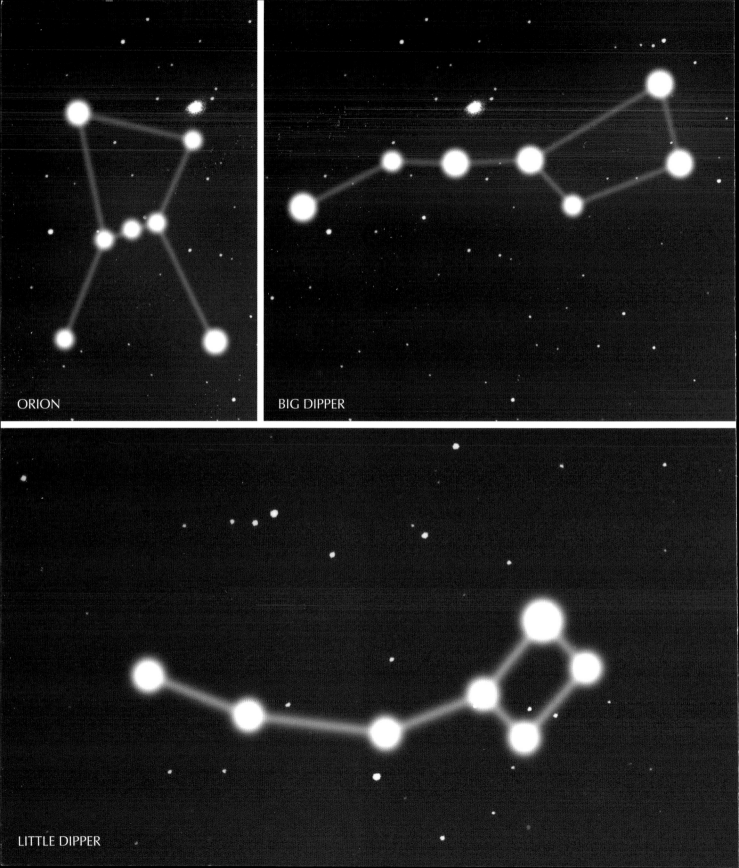

ORION

BIG DIPPER

LITTLE DIPPER

Stargazing

How many stars can you see in the night sky?

Innumerable stars shine and glitter in the night sky, making recognisable shapes called constellations. Have you ever seen Orion the Greek hunter, or Ursa Major the Great Bear? When night falls you can go on an exciting journey through the darkness. In wintertime, when the air is cold and clear, the stars are easier to identify. The best place to see them is out in the countryside, away from artificial light. In the Northern Hemisphere, on a clear night, it is possible to see approximately 2,500 stars with the naked eye.

From December to February in the Northern Hemisphere we can see the winter star signs in the eastern sky. The most well-known constellations are Auriga, Taurus, Gemini, Orion, and Canis Major and Minor. The brightest stars in these constellations form a huge hexagonal shape, known as the Winter Hexagon. Look for the most noticeable stars in the sky, connect them in your head and you will see the Winter Hexagon.

Many of the stars you see may not exist any more. Even though the star itself may have stopped shining and become extinct billions of years ago, we can still see its light. This is because light (moving at the speed of light) can take a long time to reach us across the vast expanse of space.

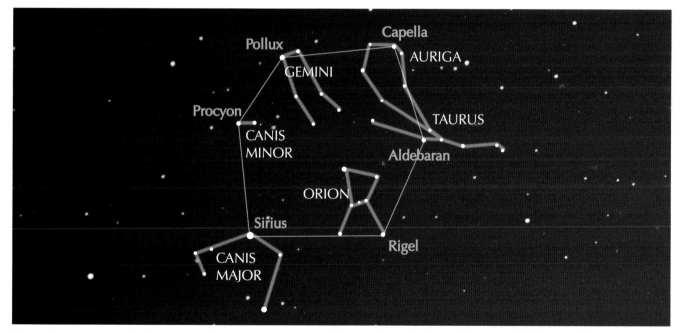

The brightest stars in the sky – Sirius, the brightest (Canis Major), Rigel (Orion), Aldebaran (Taurus), Capella (Auriga), Pollux (Gemini) and Procyon (Canis Minor) – make up the Winter Hexagon.

Using a star compass

How can we keep track of the thousands of shining dots in the sky? And how can we use them to find out where we are? Humans began to track and divide up the sky almost 4,000 years ago by giving certain star constellations the names of animals or other things. One of these is the Big Dipper, which consists of the seven brightest stars in the constellation Ursa Major (Great Bear); it looks like a cart with a handle. A little further away is a constellation named after the hunter from Greek mythology, Orion.

To use the stars as a compass, in the Northern Hemisphere, all you have to do is find the North Star (Polaris or pole star). This star shines almost directly over the North Pole and stays in the same place in the sky all through the night. Due to the way the earth rotates, all the other stars seem to move around the North Star. You can easily identify it as the last star on the handle of the Little Dipper, which is not far from the Big Dipper.

On the opposite side of the sky, to the south, the huge constellation Orion rises in the evening. This constellation has many bright stars and is the clearest constellation in the southern winter sky. Three bright stars positioned close together make up what is known as Orion's Belt.

Many other distinctive constellations to the east and west complete the sky compass. They allow us to find our way in the dark, the same way sailors have done for centuries. If you want to find out more about the starry sky, a large sky map will provide more detailed information. You could even keep your own star diary.

The distinctive constellation Orion (left) has a lot of bright stars. The Big Dipper (centre) belongs to the constellation Ursa Major. The handle of the Little Dipper (right) bends upwards with the North Star on the end.

Want to learn more about stargazing?

Read *Astronomy for Young and Old: A Beginner's Guide to the Visible Sky* by Walter Kraul

Explore the night sky with *Stargazers' Almanac: A Monthly Guide to the Stars and Planets*, published annually

What is a star?

Stars are really suns, just like our own, but further away. They are made of burning gas, emitting heat and light, and their own planets orbit around them. Planets can also look like stars, but they don't emit their own light, instead they reflect it from their sun. You can distinguish a star from a planet as the stars maintain their position in relation to each other. Also stars twinkle because they emit their own light, but planets don't.

What is a shooting star?

Shooting stars are actually meteors – huge dusty chunks of ice or rock. When they enter the atmosphere of our earth, they start to burn, so they appear to be bright falling streaks of light.

What is the Milky Way?

The Milky Way is the galaxy that our solar system is part of. A galaxy is a huge rotating disk made up of many billions of stars. Every star we can see in the night sky is part of the Milky Way. Our galaxy appears to us as a light, irregular band of stars that stretches over the entire sky, but we only get this view because we are looking at the Milky Way from the inside out. There are billions of other galaxies in the universe, but we can only see their light and stars through telescopes.

Tree Book-Box

Collect your favourite objects from trees in beautiful wooden boxes

Do you have a favourite tree? There are many species of trees to learn about in gardens and the natural world. You could even make a wooden library of tree books. You can have lots of fun gathering and drying the buds, flowers, leaves, seeds and fruit. Then make wooden 'books' to store as many parts of each tree as possible. Why not start with your favourite tree?

You will need a sturdy branch from your tree to make the spine of the book. This shows which book belongs to which tree. Have you noticed that different branches have particular characteristics? Elder branches have a soft core – marrow – and its wood turns yellow in some places when sawed in half. Lichen and moss grow on its rough bark. In contrast, hazelnut branches have thin silvery brown branches. When dried, elder wood shrinks while hazelnut branches hardly change at all.

You will need

- sheet of plywood
- small section of branch for the spine
- 2 small hinges
- small screws
- 4 brass ring screws
- brass rod for shutting the book
- wood glue or a glue gun
- ruler
- chisel, file, screwdriver, pliers, hammer, hand drill, screw clamp, saw
- fine sandpaper
- test tubes and cork stoppers
- string

Tip: Ask an adult to help you use these sharp wood-working tools.

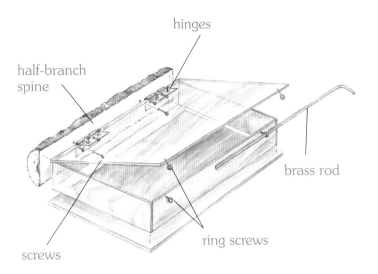

Ruler, chisel, file, screwdriver, hammer, pliers, saw and sandpaper – you will need several different tools to work with wood and metal

Decide how big you want your book-box to be and measure out the pieces onto a sheet of plywood. You will need: two front and back panels, the same size, remembering that they should overhang the sides a little; two long side panels, and two short top and bottom panels. Cut all six pieces out with a saw, then sand the corners and edges with fine sandpaper.

Glue the sides together then glue them to the back panel. Don't glue the lid, as you'll need to be able to open it. Clamp the pieces together and leave them to dry.

Measure, then use a pencil to mark where to position the hinges. Using a screwdriver, screw the hinges onto the spine-side and lid so the box opens like a book. Try to find small screws that don't stick out the other side. If they do, file them down.

Cut your branch in half vertically and then down to size to make the spine of the book. Screw it on from inside the box.

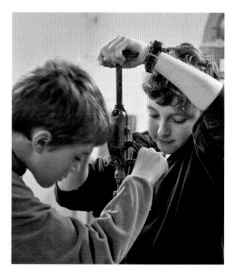

Cut the brass rod to the correct length and bend back the end. Measure, then use a pencil to mark where to position the brass ring screws: two on the underside of the lid-piece and two on the outside edge of the box. Twist the ring screws in place, making sure you can easily slide the rod through them all to shut the lid.

Once your book-box is finished, you can fill it with all the things you've collected and dried from that particular type of tree. You can use

glass test tubes, stoppered with a cork, to contain loose flowers or small fruits. You can even tie them with a length of string glued to the book. Or you can glue in roots, leaves or cross-sections of twigs. You can sketch your tree, or take photos of how it changes throughout the year, and keep these safe inside too.

What is an xylotheque?

A xylotheque is a library comprised of books made of wood, which originated in the eighteenth century. The books are hollow and contain samples of the leaves, seeds and flowers of the tree the book is made from. Xylotheque is a Greek word: *xylon* means wood and *theque* means collection. In the past, such books were made artistically and with great skill.

Feeding Garden Birds

Make feeders to attract birds to your garden in winter

Building a bird table

You will need

- strong forked branch: 180 cm (6 ft) long, 5 cm (2 in) diameter
- old wooden board: 3 cm (1 in) thick, measuring 33 x 33 cm (1 x 1 ft)
- 2 round branches for front posts: approximately 15.5 cm (6 in) long
- 2 round branches for back posts: approximately 5.5 cm (2 in) long
- 2 round branches for crossbars: approximately 60–65 cm (2 ft) long
- 2 old tiles: approximately 43 cm (1 ½ ft) long, 26 cm (11 in) wide
- drill and 10 screws: approximately 5 cm (2 in) long
- screwdriver
- screws for the tiles
- spade or trowel

Tip: Ask an adult to help you use these sharp wood-working tools.

Find a strong forked branch that you can build your bird feeder on and dig a hole approximately ½ metre (2 ft) deep. Stand the branch in it, upright, and fill the hole with soil so the post stands securely.

To make the feeder, saw the wooden board to the correct size and drill a hole in each corner where the posts will go.

Shorten the posts to their correct length and screw them to the board from the underside. Drill holes in the crossbars in the same way and screw them to the posts.

Drill holes in the board and the fork of the branch and screw the bird feeder on tight so that it doesn't move around.

Position the tiles on top of the crossbars to make the roof. Now you can put food inside for your feathered guests.

Keep your bird feeders stocked up through the winter – homemade fat balls are a delicious treat for hungry birds

Scatter seeds inside your bird table

Making a bottle feeder

You will need

- large piece of wooden board:
  2–2.5 cm (1 in) thick
- narrow pieces of wood for the frame:
  2– 2.5 cm (1 in) thick
- hammer, circular saw, bench saw, drill
- roofing felt
- screws and nails
- plastic bottle
- sharp scissors or craft knife
- pencil
- tar paper and tar paper nails

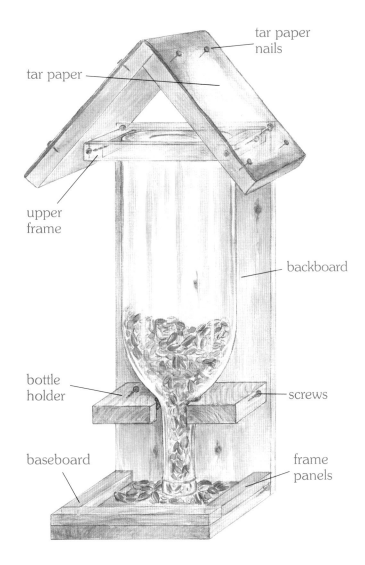

Base the measurements for your boards on the shape and size of your bottle. Sketch the shape of the backboard, roof tiles, baseboard and bottle holder onto the wooden board, measure them accurately and cut them out.

Cut a hole in the bottom of your bottle so you can refill it.

Measure, saw and nail together three narrow frame pieces to fit the baseboard and stop the food falling off. Drill holes into the backboard to attach the baseboard and the upper frame. Then screw the baseboard in place from behind the backboard.

Measure, saw and nail together three more narrow frame pieces to make the upper frame. Screw two sides of the upper frame onto the backboard.

Saw the bottle holder out of one piece of wooden board, cutting out a keyhole to fit the bottleneck.

Screw the bottle holder to the backboard, making sure to leave a gap between the neck opening of the bottle and the baseboard so the food can spill out.

Nail the two roof panels together and cover them with tar paper to make a weatherproof roof. Screw the roof to the upper frame.

Insert your bottle and fill it with seeds.

Bird-food recipes

Making fat and seed mix

You will need

- pan
- unsalted fat such as coconut oil, suet or lard
- mixed seeds and nuts
- wooden spoon

Soften hard, unsalted fat like coconut oil, suet or lard on a low heat in a pan until you can knead it. Don't let it get too hot or you will burn your hands. Mix seeds and chopped nuts into the fat until it feels coarsely grained.

Filling food baskets

You will need

- fat and seed mix
- small woven basket or half a coconut shell
- string, twine or ribbon
- scissors

Use your hands to smooth the fat and seed mix into a small woven basket or half a coconut shell.

Cut a length of twine or string and tie it to the top of the basket. You will need to make a hole in the coconut shell to thread the string through. Tie your food basket to a high bush or tree in your garden.

Hang your basket on a branch and wait, standing very still below, to see who visits

Making nut cookies

You will need

- coconut oil or lard
- peanuts or other nuts
- cookie cutters
- wooden board
- string, twine or ribbon

Place the cookie cutters onto a wooden board and fill each one with the fat. Press nuts into the fat then spread another layer of fat over the top.

Place the board in a fridge or freezer to chill until the cookie is hard.

Thread ribbon, twine or string through the top of the cookie and hang it on a tree outside.

Tip: Avoid hanging up nut cookies in spring or summer: the warm weather will melt the fat and young chicks might choke on the nuts.

Stuffing pine cones

You will need

- pine cones
- berries and seeds
- string

Collect some pine cones and keep them indoors. After a few days the scales will open in the warmth.

Add extra food for the birds by putting berries and seeds inside the scales, then tie string to the top of the cone and hang it in a tree.

Making a bell feeder

You will need

- small clay pot
- stick, the same diameter as the hole in the pot
- fat and seed mix
- 2 smaller sticks
- string

Push the thicker stick into the hole in the bottom of the clay pot. The branch should completely close the pot's hole.

Fill the pot with fat and seed mix, and push the two smaller sticks into the mixture for birds to hang on to.

Leave the pot outside to cool. Once ready, use string to tie the pot upside down in a tree like a bell.

Making a fat-seed cone

You will need

- fat and seed mix (or separate fat and birdseed)
- pine cones
- string or twine
- branches and berries to decorate

Collect some pine cones and keep them indoors. After a few days the scales will open in the warmth. Spread the fat and seed mix into the open scales.

Alternatively, you can heat coconut fat, suet or lard and dip the pine cone into it from both sides, then dip it in birdseed.

Leave it to cool and harden. Decorate it with branches and berries before tying on string to hang it up.

Choosing a good bird-feeding spot

The best place for feeding birds is in a nature garden. If you place your feeder among berry bushes and perennials you will get a lot of visitors. Birds also eat insects and grubs in piles of leaves, cracks in dry-stone walls and among branches. Placing your feeder near a pond or running water will allow birds to bathe and drink.

If you can, position your bird feeder in an elevated spot so birds can keep a lookout for predators. If you place it close enough to your window, you will be able to see the birds feeding from indoors, but be far enough away not to scare them.

Don't put too much food on your feeder at any one time, and make sure you sweep old food away regularly.

Who stays over winter and what do they eat?

Birds that overwinter in their breeding grounds are called 'resident' or 'sedentary' birds. Migrating birds fly south and partial migrants move to warmer areas only if food is sparse or the climate too rough.

Resident birds like to eat corn, or soft food such as oats, bran and raisins. Soft-food eaters like oats soaked in cooking oil, while corn eaters have a strong beak to crack hard seeds and kernels. Other birds prefer small seeds. Some soft-food eaters are omnivores and particularly enjoy fat-corn mixtures, which give them lots of energy in the cold winter.

Tip: Don't leave salty or spicy leftover food on your bird feeder. Bread and cake are also unsuitable for birds.

Garden bird visitors

Over winter you will get to know the birds that feed in your garden. You can study the different species from your window using a bird book to identify them. Soon you will understand their characteristic movements: the blackbird hops or runs over the ground; the twitchy robin flits onto the roof of the feeder before it starts to pick; tits often hang on a branch like acrobats or swing on a fat ball. The following birds are common in Europe:

The *chaffinch* is a partial migrant. It eats seeds with a short, strong beak and its favourite food is sunflower seeds.

Blue tits and *marsh tits* enjoy insects, seeds, berries and fruit. These resident birds are common guests at garden bird feeders.

Tree sparrows and *house sparrows* are sedentary birds. They often inspect a bird feeder in groups, then eat seeds and other food that has fallen down onto the ground.

The small, lively *wren* likes to make its nest in thick damp undergrowth full of herbs. It eats small insects and soil creatures, and will be attracted to a feeder by seeds and soft food. It is a partial migrant but usually overwinters at home in our latitude.

The *blackbird* likes feasting on worms and other soil animals, as well as on berries and fruit. They particularly enjoy soft apples, raisins and grain flakes in winter.

The pretty *robin* is a partial migrant which eats soil creatures, small insects and vegetables, as well as soft food and small seeds.

Bird House

Build a nesting box for blue tits

Blue tits are early risers and one of the first species of bird to nest in early spring. They collect moss, grass, hair and feathers to make their nest in March or, at the latest, April. Sometimes, if they are unlucky, a great tit or another larger hole-nesting bird will build over the blue tits' nest and oust them from their home.

You can help out these little birds by making a special nesting box with an entrance that's just the right size. By carefully building, hanging up and caring for the nesting box you can ensure that the birds are safe and warm. Clean out your nesting box in autumn, once the baby birds have fledged, by sweeping out the old nesting material with a rough brush; this removes bugs and provides a clean space to build a new nest in spring.

Tip: Ask an adult to help you use these sharp wood-working tools.

You will need

- rough wooden board: approximately 2–2.5 cm (1 in) thick
- 2 slabs of tree trunk with bark for the roof
- birch branches: approximately 3–5 cm (1–2 in) in diameter
- slat of wood for hanging: 2 cm (1 in) thick, 4 cm (1 ½ in) wide
- moss
- hammer
- drill with hole saw
- hand saw or circular saw
- nails: 4–6 cm (1 ½–2 in) long
- wood glue
- screws and aluminium nails
- sandpaper or wood file

Measurements

roof slabs: 20 x 18 cm (8 x 7 in)
front and back sections: 35 x 25 cm (12 x 10 in)
floor: 25 x 11 cm (10 x 4 in)
sides: 18 x 11 cm (7 x 4 in)
hanging slat: 60 cm (2 ft) long

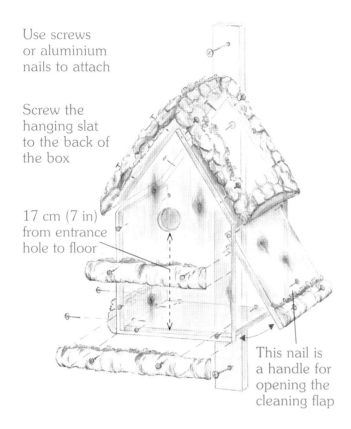

Use screws
or aluminium
nails to attach

Screw the
hanging slat
to the back of
the box

17 cm (7 in)
from entrance
hole to floor

This nail is
a handle for
opening the
cleaning flap

tit and 28 mm (1⅛ in) for a coal tit. If you want
to build a box for a great tit or nuthatch you will
need a 32 mm (1 ¼ in) hole, and for sparrows,
35 mm (1 ¼ in). Sand around the hole with the
sandpaper or a wood file.

Screw or nail the box pieces together. Attach
the cleaning flap, screwing it shut at the bottom
for now; you can unscrew it later to clean it.

If you want, you can decorate the box with birch
branches cut in half vertically and pieces of moss.

Measure and draw the floor, sides, front and back
sections onto the rough board and saw them out.

Nail together the roof slabs at approximately a
90° angle.

The distance between the lower edge of the
entrance hole and the floor of the nesting box
should be at least 17 cm (7 in) so cats can't
reach baby birds with their paws. Using rough,
unplaned wood helps baby birds to grip and
climb out more easily.

Cut the entrance hole with the burr attachment
of the drill. It should be 26 mm (1 in) for a blue

Hang the nesting box at least 2 ½ m (8 ft) high in a tree

81

Choir of Angels

Make a decorative display of angels

You will need

- newspaper
- cardboard
- wooden logs
- bowl of water
- sheet plaster of Paris (available in most craft shops)
- styrofoam balls
- long nails
- hammer
- pencil
- scissors
- hand drill
- glue
- ivy leaves, straw, hay or thick garden twine
- pot filled with sand

Cover your table with newspaper to protect it, as this is a very messy project.

Choose a log of wood to be your angel's body, preferably one that's slightly wider at the bottom to look like a robe. A twisted log will make the angel look like it's dancing.

Using your log as a size guide, draw the angel's wings onto cardboard and cut them out.

Cut the plaster strips into small pieces and dip them in water. Carefully smooth them onto the cardboard. If you can still see the cardboard, add a second layer of plaster. Leave the wings in a warm place – perhaps near an oven – on a strong piece of cardboard to dry.

Press a long nail through a styrofoam ball so that the point comes out the other side. Plaster the styrofoam ball; this will be your angel's head. Leave it to dry standing up in a pot of sand.

Once the wings are dry, nail them to the log, making sure the wing tips extend above the wood.

Drill a hole in the top of the log where you want the head to go. Push the nail in so that it holds firm. If you want the head to be extra secure, squeeze glue into the drill hole before you insert the nail.

Stand your head in a pot filled with sand to keep it steady while you cover it in plaster

What kind of crown will you make for your angel?

Every angel needs a crown. Wind one out of ivy leaves, straw, hay or thick garden twine and carefully tie it in place at three or four places around the crown.

Place the finished choir on a windowsill, light some candles and wait for night to fall.

Use a needle and thread to string together a crown of ivy leaves

Paper Angels

Fold small angels to decorate a festive window

You can use different types of paper for your angels. Tracing paper (or any other kind of transparent paper) is particularly beautiful as light shines through it. The smaller the rectangle and the finer the pleated folds, the fuller the skirt will appear.

You will need

* tracing paper or other craft paper
* wooden, glass or ceramic beads
* gold wire or thread
* glue
* sewing needle
* scissors

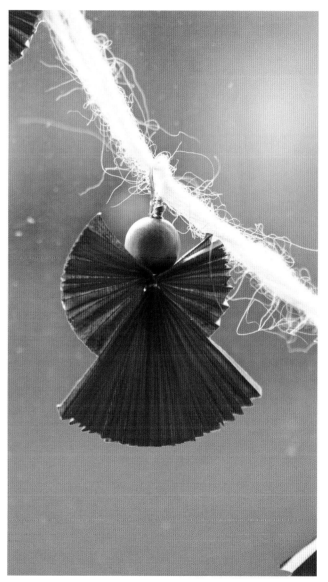

Make an angel garland by attaching your decorations to fluffy wool, twine or ribbon and hanging them up

Method 1

1. Cut your chosen paper into two different-sized rectangles – a small one for the wings and a larger one for the skirt.

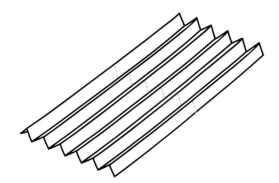

2. Fold the larger rectangle into several pleats, and fold in half.

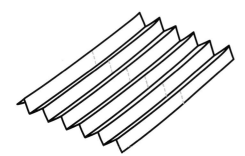

3. Fold the smaller rectangle into several pleats, and fold in half.

4. Push a needle through both centre folds to make a hole for the thread or wire to go through, then push the wire or thread through the hole. Glue the bottom fan together in the centre to make a full skirt. Next, thread a bead on to make a head.

5. Tie a knot above the bead and make a loop to hang it up with. If you're using wire, bend it into a loop and twist directly above the head until secure.

Method 2

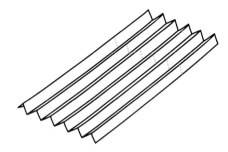

1. Fold two rectangles of the same size into several pleats, and fold about two thirds up.

3. Wind wire around the waist fold.

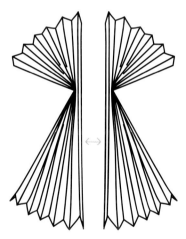

2. Glue the fans together lengthwise up to the waist fold to make the skirt.

4. Glue the lower sides of the wings to the skirt. Bend the wire up and thread on a bead for a head.

5. Make a wire loop above the head then twist directly above the head until secure.

Wrapping Gifts

Use fabric sacks to wrap your presents – just like Santa Claus

Sewing gift bags

You will need

- hessian (sackcloth) or leftover fabric
- scissors
- needle and thread
- string, ribbon or embroidery thread to decorate
- glue
- thin bark, berries, leaves, gingerbread to decorate
- thin wire

Cut out two rectangles in whatever size you would like your bag to be. Remember to leave a small seam allowance on each edge. Sew the rectangles together around the sides and bottom, then turn the bag inside out to hide the seam.

If you're using patterned fabric, sew the rectangles together with the patterned sides facing each other, so the pattern is visible when turned the right way.

Tie your bags at the top with ribbon, string or embroidery thread and add a garland of berries or beads. You can make a garland by threading berries or beads onto wire and twisting the ends together to secure the loop. Leave enough wire to attach the garland to the ribbon or string. Or cut stars or Christmas trees out of thin bark and glue them to kitchen twine, which you can use to

tie up your gift bags. Why not hang a homemade gingerbread letter as a tag so that everyone knows who your gift is for?

Making snowflake wrapping paper

You will need

- white paper
- coloured paper
- compass
- pencil
- glue

Using the compass, draw different sized circles onto white paper and cut them out with scissors.

Fold each paper circle at least twice: first in half, then in half again. The more you fold the circle, the finer the detail on the snowflake will be. Cut different patterns into the edges of the paper and unfold it to reveal your snowflake!

Glue them to coloured paper to make snowflake wrapping paper for your Christmas gifts.

Finish your gift with white lace, string or ribbon and cut out a gift tag from leftover paper

Felt Snowmen

Sew smiling snowmen to sit on a wintery windowsill

You will need

- white felt: approximately 30 × 32 cm (1 x 1 ft)
- coloured felt: approximately 16 × 18 cm (6 ¼ x 7 in)
- scraps of coloured felt
- waterproof black pen
- craft glue
- cotton wool or unspun sheep's wool for stuffing
- embroidery thread and needle
- sewing thread and needle
- pins
- tracing paper and pencil
- scissors

Use a photocopier to double the size of the snowman body template (see p.95) and cut it out. The template already has a seam allowance.

Fold a piece of white felt in half and lay the template on top. Secure it with pins, then cut out the snowman's front and back body pieces.

Sew them together around the edge with running stitch to tack them in place, then use backstitch to sew them properly. Leave the bottom of the snowman open for stuffing. Unpick the running stitch once you have sewn your backstitch seam, then turn it inside out.

To make the snowman's hat follow the same method as you did for the body, but using the hat template and a different colour of felt. Leave the bottom of the hat open.

Stuff the body and hat evenly with cotton wool or sheep's wool, but do not sew the seams shut!

Put the hat on the snowman and, if necessary, sew it to the sides of the head.

Cut the snowman's scarf out of leftover scraps of coloured felt. Wind it around the snowman's neck, gluing it on if you wish.

Draw on eyes, mouth and buttons with a waterproof black pen, or sew on real buttons. If you like, you can make a small pointed cone out of orange felt and sew or glue it on, for a carrot nose.

How to sew...
Running stitch

Bring the needle up through the fabric (1).

Then push the needle back down into the fabric from the top after the desired stitch length (2).

Bring the needle back up through the fabric after the same distance as the first stitch (3).

Continue working with even stitches. If you embroider back in the same way but offset (stitching the thread over the fabric where before it was under the fabric and vice versa), you will get an even line that looks the same as backstitch.

Backstitch

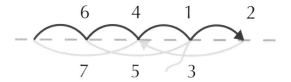

Bring the needle up through the fabric (1).

Then push the needle back down into the fabric after the desired stitch length (2). This is the first stitch.

Sew back the way you came, double the length of your stitch (3), and push the needle up through the fabric (4).

Push the needle back into the fabric at the start of your first stitch (1). This makes the second stitch.

Then push the needle down through the fabric, and sew back again, double the length of your stitch (5). Push up through the fabric (6) and back down (4) to complete your third stitch.

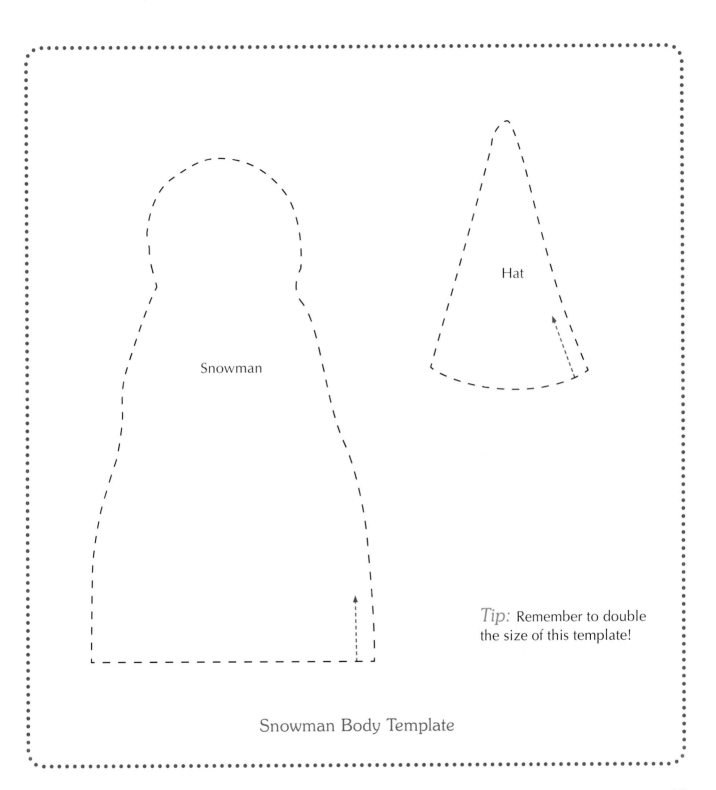

Hat

Snowman

Tip: Remember to double the size of this template!

Snowman Body Template

Fun in the Snow

Play games and build figures in crisp white landscapes

The best snow for playing with is 'sticky snow', but not every type of snow sticks together well. Sub-zero temperatures lead to powdery snow, and snowballs made from it will fall apart. Large wet snowflakes fall in slightly warmer, damper weather, and this snow is great for making snowmen, snowballs, igloos or snow animals. Seeds lie under the blanket of snow, waiting for the warmer weather of spring; the snow protects them from freezing.

Tip: Always wear warm, waterproof clothes and shoes when playing in the snow.

Building a snowman

You will need

- snow!
- carrots
- chestnuts, stones, potatoes or coal for eyes and buttons
- old scarf and hat
- twigs

Sticky snow is best for building snowmen! Start by making a small snowball in your hands, then roll it round and round on the ground so that it gets bigger and bigger as it picks up snow. As it grows, the ball will become quite heavy – you may need all your strength to move it! Make a smaller ball for the head and stack it on top of the body.

A snowman needs buttons, eyes and a mouth. Make them with pieces of coal, conkers, stones or potatoes. Add a carrot nose, a scarf and an old hat for its head. Make snow arms and hands from twigs, and add any other details you like.

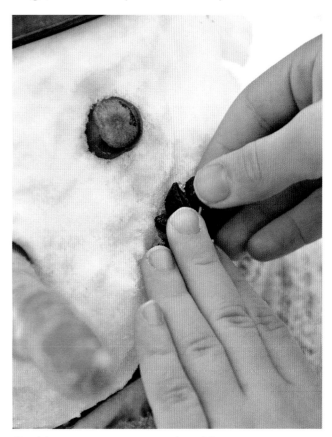

Coal buttons, a warm scarf and hat, a carrot nose, conker eyes, pine-cone ears and aniseed cheeks

Making a snow spider and hedgehog

- sticks
- stones, walnuts or conkers

For the spider, roll a small ball for the head and a large ball for the body. Attach the head to the body with more snow. Break eight long sticks in half to make jointed legs. Use smaller sticks for feelers and stones, walnuts or conkers for eyes.

For the hedgehog, make a large ball for the body, and shape one end into a point for the face. Push in lots of sticks for spines. Use stones, walnuts or conkers for the eyes and snout.

Hedgehogs are very spiky, so the more sticks you use, the better!

Oops! This snow spider has lost two legs! Make sure yours has eight like a real spider

Running a snow maze

Find a large patch of snow without any tracks. Stand alongside your friends in a straight line, then run to the other side of the space, criss-crossing back and forth all the way to make a confusing maze. Once you all reach the other side, swap places with the person next to you and try to find your way back as quickly as possible. The first one back is the winner.

Playing snow marbles

You will need

❀ marbles or wooden beads

Build a cone shape out of snow. Using your finger or a stick, make tracks that criss-cross down to the bottom and roll your marbles down the track. The marbles will roll quickly down steep parts, and slower on more level parts. You could even build a tunnel for them to run through.

Playing snow trains

Stand in a line one behind another, each holding onto the shoulders or waist of the person in front. Slide your feet forwards through the snow as if on a train track: first the right foot, then the left. With enough children you can make two trains and race each other.

Bowling pine cones

You will need

❀ 10 large round pine cones

Stand the pine cones in a triangle shape – as you would with skittles. Stand about 2 m (6 ft) away and take turns trying to hit them with snowballs. When you start to get better, move further back and keep trying. The winner is the one who can hit the pine cones from furthest away.

Sledging

Sledge solo or see how many you can fit on one sledge. The snowy slope will get faster the more you sledge down it. If you're brave enough, try lying on your stomach to race down the slope. You can also tie sledges together and slide down in a train. Perhaps you could have a race and see who has the fastest sledge, or build a jump out of snow and sledge right over it?

Making snow angels

Lie on your back in the snow! Wave your arms and legs back and forth to make the wings and robe of an angel. Make several for a whole choir of snow angels!

Tip: Once you've finished playing in the snow, go inside and warm up with a hot drink.

Which tracks in the snow belong to which animal?

Many animals leave tracks in the white untouched snow, which you can investigate. Follow a deer track or discover the tracks of a fox hunting a mouse. If you come across gnawed pine cones, perhaps you can identify which animal ate them?

Hare

Blackbird

Hares and rabbits bound across fields, leading with their back legs, which you will see before their front legs.

Blackbirds only leave delicate impressions as they hop lightly over the snow.

Wild boar

Mice

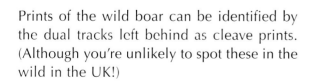

Prints of the wild boar can be identified by the dual tracks left behind as cleave prints. (Although you're unlikely to spot these in the wild in the UK!)

You can see a line where the tail drags along the ground between the fine paw tracks.

Deer

Deer leave cloven-hooved tracks in the snow.

Fox

From a distance, a fox's paw tracks look like a string trail in the snow.

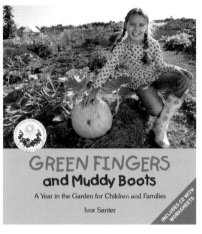
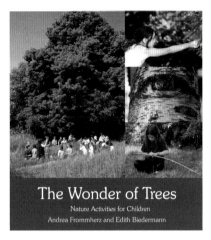
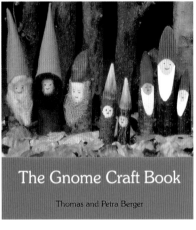
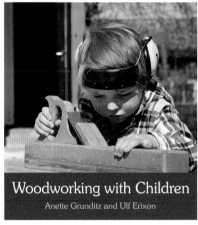